25
EXERCISES
TO
STRENGTHEN
YOUR
PARENTING MUSCLES

CHINENYE O. OPARAH

&

KIA M. HASELRIG-OPARAH

Dedication

To our families and our heroes...
who are often the same people.

Foreword

—∿∿—

Have you ever stared wide-eyed and a bit shocked at your child and wondered aloud, "Where in the world is the manual?" Thinking to yourself that it was only a few years ago that you were a stubborn adolescent yourself and now, in an astonishing turn of events, you are responsible for guiding tiny little humans through childhood, adolescence and on to nothing short of greatness? If so, this book is for you.

Anyone who said parenting is a piece of cake was never a parent. While we all have our days where we feel like the Michael Jordan or Mother Teresa of parenting – completely on top of our game and making an incredible difference in the lives of our tiny humans, we quite possibly more often feel like we are flying by the seat of our pants, just a little (or even a lot) unsure of what to do next. And so we turn to parenting books hoping that someone has discovered the magic formula and that, much like arithmetic, if we study it long and hard enough, we will master it, apply it with grace and be able to sit back and enjoy the fruits of our labor. Unfortunately, often when we open those books, rather than finding the peace and knowledge we seek, we are instead inundated with so many things we are not doing and even more things that we couldn't even begin to imagine adding to our overly busy schedules that we begin to wonder if being a great parent isn't some unicorn of an idea that only happens in Never Never Land.

Well, lucky for us, 25 Exercises to Strengthen Your Parenting Muscles, is just the book we have been looking for. I will even go so far as to say it has the magic formula – 25 of them, in fact! Written by Kia Haselrig-Oparah, a mother, psychologist, education enthusiast, author, and Chinenye Oparah, a father, engineer, educator, author, and both of whom are my friends, this book is chock full of 25 challenges to enhance your parenting style. Now, you may think – twenty-five? Twenty-five? Yes, there are twenty-five challenges. At only one challenge per week (if only parenting were as easy as arithmetic), unlike other parenting guides, this does not assume you will be able to add all 25 to your already busy lives. Just try each one on for size - for one week. If it works for you, perfect! If not, there will surely be one or more that does.

For that reason, I really enjoyed this book.

I especially like the first challenge – "Talk to your child, instead of on your cell phone, while driving in the car." Given my absolute love of making every minute count, this turns what could be a lost 20 minutes in traffic into a meaningful chance to find out what happened in school today and how my sons felt about it. The friendly language and supportive approach of the book turns what could be an overwhelming list of "shoulds" into a very doable list of "coulds."

Dive right in and start designing your own magic formula for this thing called parenting.   Consider 25 Exercises to Strengthen Your Parenting Muscles a personal trainer of sorts – there to give you ideas when you've run out and pat you on the back when you've had a Hall of Fame Parenting Day.

Enjoy!
Nzinga A. Harrison, M.D.
Psychiatrist

Introduction

I suspect we aren't the only parents who think our children are brilliant, beautiful, and spectacular in every way. As parents, it seems logical that we are allowed to think highly of our children. Realistically, we know we have a ten-year-old girl and a two-year-old boy who are special in many ways and are also typical children in many other ways.

As educators and through our work in the nonprofit world, we have experienced the joys of education from children ranging in intellectual capacity. One thing that has been consistent in our work with children is the idea that each child deserves every opportunity to achieve his highest potential. The best way to encourage the love of learning is to start early and make learning fun. Early can mean different things to different people. For us, we started soon after we found out we were pregnant. Do you think that's a tad ridiculous? It could be, but I will say that we are pleased with our progress thus far. Parenting isn't about judging other parents. Ideally, parenting works better when we work together. When there are shared experiences of what works for you and what hasn't worked. Do what words for you and your family. This will be different for many families. Diversity is a good thing.

What makes us qualified to talk about this parenting and education stuff? Chinenye teaches high school Physics and has a Systems Engineering degree from Georgia Tech. He also spent two years working at an alternative school for middle and high school students, two-years teaching high school math, and several years teaching Physics. My degree is in School Psychology and I work in that field for six years. Though I no longer work in this capacity, I do hold current certifications for school psychology in three states. I have served on the board of directors at our daughter's previous school, where she learned Japanese, since it opened in June 2012. I also have experience with individual and group counseling for children, and their families. Together, Chinenye and I have a combined 13 years of experience with a nonprofit organization that works with middle and high school students, teaching leadership skills and community service.

Our sweet ten-year old daughter, Kemery, started reading at two and a half years old. She is fluent in Japanese. Kemery loves learning and enjoys reading. Academically, she has been leaps and bounds beyond what is expected for a child her age. What about socially? Kemery enjoys cooking, singing, dancing, time with family friends, and helping others. Kemery has completed 21 races in three states. Four of the races were children's triathlons. Kemery enjoys volunteering with her church and sorting vegetables at a local vegetable co-op. Per her request, Kemery also started a business at the age of eight-years-old! Through her business, she has accomplished some tremendous feats in a short amount of time including having her clothing line on the runway of Atlantic City Fashion Week, being honored (with Mommy) in the 18th Anniversary Edition of Who's

Who in Black Atlanta, being honored by the City Council with Kemery Kreates' Appreciation Day, and being featured in several magazines including Teen Boss!

Kemery was the inspiration behind us starting our company, Raise the Bar Learning, LLC. Baby brother, Jeremy, inspires us to keep it going. Though he has a different personality, Jeremy is already following in the footsteps of his sister. He loves music, is very interested in Japanese, and loves to read! The cool part about what we do with Kemery and Jeremy is that it is replicable, it's not a secret, and we want to help guide other parents to the resources available to help challenge their own children. Raise the Bar Learning, LLC has two goals: The first goal is to help parents and educators challenge children to achieve their highest potential, in a fun way. The other goal is to activate a movement of young volunteers who will be change agents in the world. In 2012, Raise the Bar Learning, LLC's program, This Little Light, collected stickers to send to children in a Nigerian village, where Chinenye's family is from. In 2013, the children collected school supplies for the same school in Nigeria. We will offer more opportunities for children to participate in age appropriate volunteering. For example, we have also collected letters and drawings by our child volunteers, from across the nation, to send to a little girl in Texas, who had been diagnosed with cancer for the third time.

People often inquire about how we taught Kemery and Jeremy to read so early, how do they know so much, or what ideas do we have to share that may help them with their own child. That being said, we wrote this book as the follow-up to Kia's first parenting book, Parenting is a Verb: The Art of Unlocking Your Baby's Potential. For 25 Exercises to Strengthening Your Parenting Muscles, we wanted a book general enough that we could reach parents with children at varying ages and a book specific enough that parents could focus on one activity at a time to keep from feeling overwhelmed. The idea is that if we simply work on implementing one activity at a time, one week at a time, we can all sharpen our parenting skills in one way or another. Each activity is used as a guide. You are the expert for your child. If the exercise is beyond your child's level or your child is beyond the level of the activity, feel free to adapt accordingly. We want to get you thinking about what you can do to be more involved and interactive with your child. At the end of each exercise, in the book, there is space for you to journal your experience with completing the journey. Ask yourself questions to help you remember what happened through this experience. How did your children receive completing the exercise? How did they feel? How did you feel? Is this an exercise you would consider implementing into your routine (daily, weekly, monthly, or annually)?

I must add here that Kemery has been interested in editing. She feels fancy when she catches a mistake in written text and she enjoys playing an editing game on the tablet. She has even edited other published works. As we hope to encourage her to use her gifts, we hired her to edit this book. This is a prime example of there are no perfect parents. We are all doing the best we can with what we have. Wait. What? That didn't make sense, did it? Keep reading. After Kemery finished editing the book, she let us know how awesome the book was and said she had one major critique. Welcoming her feedback, we asked about the critique. She politely let us know that she was interested in all of the exercises in the book and she wondered why we had not done the exercises with her! Wow! How powerful was that critique?

We explained to Kemery that we actually had done almost all of the exercises with her, when she was much younger. However, the message it drove homehat was a reminder to us that children learn and retain information through repetition. After all of the opportunities and experiences that Kemery has been exposed to in her life, how could we possibly expect her to remember all of these without reinforcing them? We learn from our children all the time. They help us to be better parents. Given that information, we will also participate in the parenting gym by completing the 25 Exercises to Strength our Parenting Muscles, for the first time with Jeremy and for round two with Kemery. Thank you to Kemery for reminding us that part of this parenting journey is to continue reinforcing the skills, ideas, lessons, and traditions that we want our children to learn and remember.

Contents

~~~

Talk to your child, instead of on your cell phone, while driving in the car.

This first exercise is easier said than done. For one week, have conversations with your child when you are riding in the car. It's fine to keep the phone nearby in case an emergency arises, but other than that, do not accept phone calls unless absolutely necessary. If you must make or take a phone call, keep it brief--under two minutes.

Children are observing our every move and encoding our behavior into their understanding of the world. We already knew this, but it was confirmed when our daughter was about three-years-old and she told someone that Mommy was always on the computer. There is even a picture of us sitting next to each other, each using our laptops. Our daughter's laptop was a toy. When I saw that picture I realized that I was not presenting the positive image that I wanted her to have of me. I changed my behavior and made a sincere effort to mainly use the computer when she was at school or while she was asleep.

Here's another Mommy reflection. Our children are eight years apart. As I sit here typing, I must say that our son may have the same thoughts that Kemery did when she was his age. Now that I have been working from home, he often sees me at the computer. Dually noted and I will be more intentional about rewriting that narrative. Parenting is a continuous opportunity for us to check our own behavior as we hope to shape our children's behavior.

Similarly, children observe your behavior, both positive and negative, while driving. Do you "multitask" while driving? Do you use a headset while talking on the phone? Do you roll through the stop sign instead of making a complete stop? Do you have road rage? You are setting the tone for your child's future driving habits. What messages do you want to send?

Additionally, the benefit of this particular challenge is that you gain an opportunity to talk with your child, to learn more about their perspective on the world, their ability to navigate the world around them, and to let your child know that you are there for them and ready to lend a listening ear.

To fill our driving time, we take the opportunity in the car to ask our children open-ended (not "yes" or "no") questions about their day. Yes, even our two-year old can answer to some extent. His response may be, "I play with my friends," which we think is a great start. We will follow-up and prompt him to get more indepth answers.

Journal

_____

_____

_____

_____

_____

_____

_____

_____

_____

_____

_____

_____

_____

_____

_____

_____

_____

_____

Speak the way you want
your child to speak.

Talk to your child exactly the way you want him to talk to you...five years from now. You are your son's first grammar coach. You are your daughter's first vocabulary builder. If you haven't stepped up your game already, now is the time. If you have an infant or a toddler, avoid the trap of speaking like him or her. From our perspective, the only acceptable baby talk comes from a baby!

Chinenye: My dad corrected my diction and grammar throughout my childhood. It took me until I was fourteen years old when I finally caught him making a grammatical mistake. You'd think I had just won the lottery! I am articulate now because my parents were articulate then. Children learn from us all the time and continually try to grasp what is just out of reach. Often a child may not start walking until she sees other small children walking. It's as if they say to themselves, "Oh, if my friend can do that, I think I'll give it a try." If we choose to speak to them in a way that doesn't teach them, then we rob their young minds of the opportunity to extend their educational reach.

Having a little Mommy and son time last night with Jeremy, we began to build a tower with blocks. As we built the tower, between having other conversation and in a fun way, I would throw in comments like:

"Wow, this tower is getting really tall! I'll start adding more blocks to the bottom to make a solid, sturdy foundation. This tower will be very strong if the foundation is solid. We have to make the foundation, the bottom of the tower, nice and sturdy to keep the tower from toppling over. This is amazing! This tower is tall. Good thing we made a strong, sturdy foundation to support this tall tower. I like how we are using symmetry as we build this tower. You put a blue block over on this side. I'll get another blue block for you to put on the opposite side, to make it symmetrical. We have the same color on both sides. Wow! This is amazing! Look! Both sides are symmetrical! Our tower is going to be strong, sturdy, and symmetrical! You're doing a great job building this tower, Jeremy! I'm glad we can build the tower together."

To him, he was having a fun time building a tower with Mommy. To me, I was enjoying the quality time and being intentional about sowing the seed of new vocabulary. In that short dialogue, while we were playing,

Jeremy has now been exposed to seven new vocabulary words. He may not remember them all tomorrow. However, as we increase the time we spend building, he will begin to acquire the new vocabulary and even use it appropriately in his conversations with others.

Also, in that conversation, Jeremy was praised for doing a good job building. He heard I was happy to work with him. I showed him I was happy to engage in play time with him. He heard his name, Jeremy, being associated with praise and not punishment or consequence.

Here's an example of how quickly children acquire new information and apply what they learn. Kemery and I came home and went to say goodnight to Jeremy before he went to bed. He yelled with enthusiasm, "Kemery! I'm so glad to see you!" This comment did not come from one night of playing with blocks; however, openly showing appreciation for being around people who make you happy is a skill he has picked up because adults around him (home, day care, family, in the community) are consistently showing and communicating enthusiasm and pure joy when he shows up.

Keep in mind; however, that these tiny tots are still children; we need to make sure that we don't swing the pendulum too far. Sometimes they won't understand what we are saying, so we have to break down challenging concepts and constantly define new words. If your son or daughter continues to ask the meaning of some of the words you are using then you are on the right track!

Journal

No fast food.

Either make very healthy selections when eating out or simply cook at home for the week.

There has been recent research indicating that fast food has been a major challenge for adults and children alike. There has been a significant increase in obesity, childhood obesity, diabetes, different forms of cancer, and other illnesses over the years. When you drive down the street, there are multiple choices of fast food, tempting customers with easy, and supposedly inexpensive options. Is there any correlation?

Many people believe that our health is directly impacted by what we put in our bodies. Following that logic, there is a good chance that making the effort to cook more and eat out less is the ideal situation for raising healthy children and living healthier lives, at a very basic level. Quick, balanced family meals can be made at home for less than a trip to your local fast food restaurant.

Journal

_____

_____

_____

_____

_____

_____

_____

_____

_____

_____

_____

_____

_____

_____

_____

_____

Work out with your child.

Find time in your day to exercise together. Go to the park. Ride bikes. Go for a walk. Go to the playground. Play tag. You could even let your child help you create a workout with her own ideas such as 13 push-ups, seven sit-ups, 39 jumping jacks or whatever may come to mind at the time. Be flexible and have fun! Just be sure to keep it to her level so she won't get discouraged.

The best part about exercise is that the activity can vary from day-to-day. Children learn their lifestyle habits, both good and bad, from the adults around them. It is important to make sure that children are physically active. You must strike a balance between being active and being overactive. We do not want to stress children. Their bodies are still growing and are at risk of injury. Check with your child's physician prior to beginning any exercise program. Laugh often. Play. Enjoy spending time together.

Journal

_____

_____

_____

_____

_____

_____

_____

_____

_____

_____

_____

_____

_____

_____

_____

_____

Read together for thirty minutes every day.

When your tiny tot is just a baby, make sure he hears the cadence and inflection of your voice. Learning to listen to your parents starts early. As your child starts to become familiar with certain books, pause and let him fill in a word or phrase. Make sure you point to the word so he can start to recognize sentence structure and letters of words.

As your toddler grows a little older, have him try to identify sight words in books. You can always search for introductory sight words (it, is, was, the, etc) on the internet. The more words children know by sight, the closer they will get to reading sentences. Be sure to encourage him to attempt words, but remember that the activity has to be fun. You may be surprised at the speed your son or daughter is able to pick up this skill.

When their ability to read sentences is stronger, take turns reading paragraphs. Eventually your child will be reading to you for thirty minutes on most nights. I say most nights, because even when your little ones are skilled readers, they still enjoy hearing a story from Mommy or Daddy. At this point, you can switch it up and have everyone reading independently, in the same read. This allows your children to witness you prioritizing reading as well.

Journal

_____

_____

_____

_____

_____

_____

_____

_____

_____

_____

_____

CHALLENGE

Limit screen time to
thirty minutes per day.

Screen time includes television, cell phones, tablets, iPads, video games, computers, and laptops. Ideally, even ten or fifteen minutes each day would be plenty, but thirty minutes allows time for a streamed cartoon or educational show.

There was a time where we personally believed that screen time would not have a place in our home. Given the advances in technology and after viewing some of the shows available, we agreed that there were educational opportunities that might otherwise be missed.

Being flexible is a wonderful thing. Preview the games your child plays, the shows they watch, and the books they read. Make sure there is some educational component and that it is entertaining, as well as age appropriate.

Journal

_____

_____

_____

_____

_____

_____

_____

_____

_____

_____

_____

_____

_____

_____

_____

_____

Play cards or
board games as a family.

L et your child pick a game to play as a family. We like Candyland, Uno, and Old Maid. There are many matching games available as well. These games are great for families who are incorporating younger children in the family fun. We have some made-up games that evolved from games we learned on family game night over the holidays. For older children, we also enjoy building things with blocks or electric circuit kits made for children. Games that teach about money are always a hit with the children and are great tools for teaching life skills.

Allowing your daughter to select the game lets her know that her opinion is important to you. Playing games together diverts attention away from the screen time that seems to consume many children, and adults, with the shift in the access to technology. This investment in time will be memorable to your child. It also serves the purpose of giving your child options of things that she enjoys doing while waiting for you, in the future, to do something else like washing dishes or making a phone call.

Journal

_____

_____

_____

_____

_____

_____

_____

_____

_____

_____

_____

_____

_____

_____

_____

_____

_____

Let your child
help prepare dinner.

Pick a child-friendly meal and let your son help you prepare dinner. Meals like homemade pizza, macaroni and cheese, spaghetti, and slow-cooker dinners offer many opportunities to let children help. Remember that parents should handle anything requiring the use of sharp utensils, heat, or electrical appliances. Children are great at sprinkling the cheese, measuring and adding ingredients to the bowl, and stirring the ingredients. Older children, with the use of a child-friendly knife (made of a special plastic material), can be taught to help cut vegetables, while younger children can help by breaking the food with their fingers (think snap peas or green peas). Younger children are also great at helping to wash the fruits and vegetables.

Cooking together is wonderful because you can teach functional life skills in a fun way. Cooking is a sustainable skill that can be used once your little one leaves the nest and starts a life of his own. Reading, comprehension, and math skills are all necessary when following a recipe. Math is also used when creating in the kitchen. You could reinforce fractions with slices of pizza, slices of apples, or orange slices to name a few. Children learn about measurement of liquids and solids as well as about fractions when pouring dry or wet ingredients. Cooking is like chemistry with food. Knowing how seasonings and foods react when put together is what can make a meal mouth watering...or not.

Journal

_____

_____

_____

_____

_____

_____

_____

_____

_____

_____

Go for a walk after dinner.

After dinner, weather permitting, go for a short walk or a long walk. If there is a safe park nearby, walk to the park and play with your children before walking back.

Going for a walk after dinner is actually a great habit that promotes healthy living. Being outside helps children to digest the food that was just eaten, breathe fresh air, and use up some extra energy prior to bedtime. The goal of all of these exercises is to spend more time with your child. Yes, the sacrifice of time can be taxing on us as parents but the short- and long-term rewards far outweigh any temporary inconvenience.

Journal

_____

_____

_____

_____

_____

_____

_____

_____

_____

_____

_____

_____

_____

_____

_____

_____

_____

_____

_____

_____

_____

_____

10

Ask about school with open-ended questions.

Put the phone down and walk away from the computer. Instead, take the time to learn from your child. Let him be the expert on his day. Be actively engaged in what he says about the day. Ask questions. Be present and available to hear what your child reports happened at school.

We like to give our children an opportunity to talk about their day. We started this practice of talking about our day as soon as they could talk. Why? Think about it. We sent Kemery to school when she was only thirteen-months-old. Jeremy went to school sooner than that, though not for long. It was very convenient for us to have a children who can clearly articulate what happened at school. Their ability to summarize the day helps us to follow-up with situations that arise at school, keep abreast of the latest friendship celebrations and woes, and monitor academics. There is a sense of comfort in knowing that your child can state their feelings at school and at home as well as being able to articulate any concerns or worries. For the record, our daughter was not able to clearly articulate her day at thirteen-months-old. Neither was our son. They were both able to communicate via sign language at that time though. Now that both of our children are a little older, we ask more detailed questions about their day and we expect more than simply a "fine" or "good" response.

Here are a few of the questions we ask on a daily basis.

- "What is one skill you learned today?" (We ask this for each of our daughter's classes.)

- "What is something fun that you did today?"

- "Was anyone mean to you today?" If the answer is "yes," then we talk about that further.

- "Was anyone nice to you today?" If the answer is "yes," then we talk about how that made them feel and how they can make others feel the same way when they choose to be kind to others.

- "Did you get into trouble today?" If the answer is "yes," then we talk about what happened before and after they got into trouble. We talk about the consequences and how it made them feel. We discuss what could be done differently to prevent getting into trouble in the future. Then, unless the offense was truly serious, move on. Apply timely consequences when appropriate. The point is that you want your child to feel comfortable telling you anything and everything without unnecessary repercussions.

- "Did you help anyone today?" (i.e. Pick up a pencil that a classmate dropped or hold the door open for a friend?) Sometimes a child will say they did not help anyone. When this happens, dig deeper. Did your child help the teacher by following the rules and therefore being a good role model for other children to do the same?

Journal

_____

_____

_____

_____

_____

_____

_____

_____

_____

_____

_____

_____

Think about the number of times you ask your child's opinion. Increase the number of opportunities you allow for your child to share her thoughts.

Ask your child's opinion on various topics. Maybe you could let your child pick out the vegetable for dinner. Ask about his opinion regarding which color napkins to buy.

Think about what your work life would be like if your boss made all the decisions that impact you and never asked your opinion. How would that make you feel? It is empowering to feel as though your opinion matters and that your ideas are being considered. Teaching your child that his opinion is valued sets the stage for allowing him to feel comfortable coming to you when there are concerns in the future. Children will also feel confident to make other decisions when they are older. Open lines of communication are critical in the success of childhood transitions.

Journal

_____

_____

_____

_____

_____

_____

_____

_____

_____

_____

_____

_____

_____

_____

_____

_____

_____

12

Ask what your child likes to do and what makes her happy.

Many times we make assumptions about what children want and what they like based on our experiences with them. Sometimes we forget to ask the child's opinion as we plan activities. That can be okay in many cases but remember to sometimes include your child when you're making plans that affect her.

We usually like to do something nice for our daughter's birthday. We plan the entire party, on a budget of course, and she has a blast. Last year we were headed in the same direction but decided to ask her opinion about what she wanted to do for her birthday. She had a very thoughtful response which actually turned out to be less expensive than what we were planning. She had an amazing party that she felt good about. When given the opportunity, children can really surprise you with their ideas. Let your child think and let her know that you value her opinion.

Journal

_____

_____

_____

_____

_____

_____

_____

_____

_____

_____

_____

_____

_____

_____

_____

13

Talk about different professions.

You take your daughter to the doctor but does she know the doctor is called a pediatrician? You take your son to pick up his new glasses. Does he know he is going to see an obstetrician? Does your son know that the building where he learns each day was designed by an architect? Take the time to talk about the professionals who are involved in making your world operate each day.

Do not be afraid to use big words with children. They can handle it. When you do use larger words you may have to define them to make sure your child understands what you are saying. You may have to offer examples. Defining words and providing examples will become a natural way of life when you practice doing that on a day-to-day basis.

Journal

_____

_____

_____

_____

_____

_____

_____

_____

_____

_____

_____

_____

_____

_____

_____

_____

_____

_____

_____

_____

_____

14

Do crafts together.

Consider yourself crafty? Great! This is right up your alley. Not so crafty? No problem, that's why we have the internet or better yet...the library! Do not be afraid to make a mess. Color, cut, paste, draw, paint, make, and build!

Doing crafts helps children to develop their fine motor skills (such as using scissors) as well as their creativity. Do not obsess over perceived mistakes or make a big deal about imperfections. Why? It's art! Besides, your child is watching and learning how to handle different situations based on the behaviors you display. Please, let loose and have fun with this one!

Journal

_____

_____

_____

_____

_____

_____

_____

_____

_____

_____

_____

_____

_____

_____

_____

_____

_____

_____

_____

_____

_____

Make a schedule that include play as well as responsibilities.

Set up a calendar that is child friendly. For young children, use pictures. For older children use pictures, words, or both to identify the tasks that need to be accomplished on a daily basis. There should be time scheduled for chores as well as for play. As always, the tasks should be age appropriate. There could be time scheduled for story time, morning chores (then clearly define what the chores are such as making the bed, brushing teeth, or putting backpack by the door), and outside time.

Children respond well to structure, but be careful not to be too rigid and take away your child's ability to be flexible. Talk about how the schedule is only a guide and that things may change. Give examples of how things could change. For example, the schedule may have outside time but it could change because there may be a thunderstorm that day. Talk about what it means to be flexible and remind your son that he is capable of thinking of other things to do when the schedule has to change.

Journal

_____

_____

_____

_____

_____

_____

_____

_____

_____

_____

_____

_____

_____

Practice setting boundaries at work to protect your home life.

This one is tricky. Generally, we need income to sustain our lifestyle. Making waves with the boss or at the job is not a favorable idea and we are not suggesting that you do that. Sometimes there is some room for discussion or flexibility. When possible, make your family life a priority by establishing clear boundaries at work. For example, if you have work that you take home, consider doing the work after your daughter goes to sleep. If you have a work phone, let coworkers know you will be unavailable between the hours that your child gets home and bedtime or that you will have the phone off every night at dinnertime.

In many cases, work is not a flexible situation. Don't put your job at risk. Simply do what you can.

Journal

_____

_____

_____

_____

_____

_____

_____

_____

_____

_____

_____

_____

_____

_____

_____

_____

_____

_____

_____

_____

_____

_____

Tell your child you think they are awesome.

How many ways can you tell your child how cool he is this week? Let's find out! Be genuine but really step up the amount of times that you actually communicate how much you enjoy being around him.

What would it do for you if your co-workers, boss, friends, or family members told you how much they enjoy your company and appreciate what you bring to the relationship be it professional, personal, or romantic? People like to feel appreciated, loved, and awesome! Enough said.

Journal

_____

_____

_____

_____

_____

_____

_____

_____

_____

_____

_____

_____

_____

_____

_____

_____

_____

_____

_____

_____

_____

_____

18

Make time for yourself.

There are twenty-four hours in a day and you certainly deserve to have one of those hours just for you. Finding the time to take for yourself will contribute to you being a better parent.

We really wanted to exercise but could not figure out how to fit going to the gym into our budget or going running into our schedule. Neither one of us are "morning people." However, we knew that if we were going to fit in time for ourselves, we would have to sacrifice somewhere. Ultimately we ended up waking up between 4:00am and 5:00am to fit in our workouts. At first it was really hard. Then it became necessary. That time was dedicated to doing something for ourselves. We use workout videos during the cold months and in the warmer months we take turns going for early morning runs, usually with a running group for safety.

Exercise might not be your "thing" but be sure to find some time in the day for yourself, whether it is reading, cooking, or just talking on the phone with a friend.

Journal

_____

_____

_____

_____

_____

_____

_____

_____

_____

_____

_____

_____

_____

_____

_____

_____

_____

Family chores and cleaning.

Dedicate time to clean together. Even younger children can help. Younger children can sweep with the little broom, they can wipe off the kitchen table with a wet cloth, and they can pick up their toys. Be creative to find a way to get everyone involved.

You might wonder, "What is the point of having younger children involved with cleaning when you will have to go back and clean that part over again?" First, resist the urge to re-clean in front of your child. The point is not for the chore to be done to perfection. The point is to teach responsibility, to teach life skills, and to make sure that everyone in the family knows that it is their duty to be a contributing member of the family. Chores are not to be used as a method of punishment. Small children want to help and want to do what their parents do. Give them something age appropriate to do. You could help them with that chore or have them work on that while you handle another chore. Keep them in sight though. Safety is always a priority. When everyone pitches in, the work gets done faster and everyone is responsible for the family's living space.

Allowance? We weren't a fan of that idea initially but if there are chores that are regular and expected and those chores are complete, then chores beyond the usual and customary could be negotiated for a small allowance. We like the idea of allowance for the purpose of teaching functional skills such as money counting, saving money, and financial responsibility.

Journal

_____

_____

_____

_____

_____

_____

_____

_____

_____

_____

_____

_____

Create an appreciation basket or jar.

Decorate an empty jar, cup, box, or basket and make some time at the end of each day to write something that you are grateful for that happened during the day. If you have older children, you may consider a more advanced method by writing down something you are grateful for first thing in the morning! Put the slips of paper in the appreciation jar each day. Every so often, take out the slips and remind each other of the wonderful things that have happened in your lives.

Practicing anything is the key to improving and getting better. The same goes for being appreciative. When you practice seeing the positive in different situations, you learn to be more thankful across the board.

Journal

_____

_____

_____

_____

_____

_____

_____

_____

_____

_____

_____

_____

_____

_____

_____

_____

_____

_____

_____

_____

_____

Eat dinner together.

At dinner time, sit down together, making sure to keep the television off and the cell phones out of sight. If this is a new practice, it may be awkward at first. Do not be discouraged. It gets more comfortable with time and the benefits are quite rewarding.

See if you can eat dinner together every night for at least a week. Aim for five days of family dinners from Sunday to Thursday and even if you only get three or four (that is more than you did before), then you've succeeded. Of course it's difficult with our busy schedules, after-school activities, homework, and everything else we have on our agendas. All that does not take away from the fact that a family needs some communion time. Think of it like exercising: if we don't make time to be healthy, we'll have to take time to be sick. Eating together is another type of health. It's the way we can check on each other and see how we're all doing at one time.

Chinenye: When I was growing up, my dad even insisted that there be no talk of business at the table: no deadlines, or bills or obligations--just catching up with each other and recounting events of the day as well as sparking interesting conversation.

Journal

_____

_____

_____

_____

_____

_____

_____

_____

_____

_____

_____

_____

_____

_____

From after-school to bedtime, be present, and available.

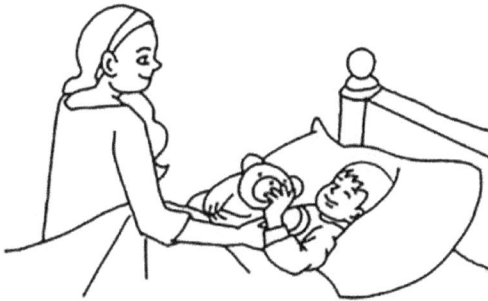

Leave work at work and live in the moment when you have the privilege of spending time with your child during the week. Pretend you are on a plane taking off: stow your smartphones, electronic devices and other distractions until you've reached cruising altitude after bedtime.

Most of us--at least for a moment at work--wish we could spend more quality time with our children. During the week, by the time we get home from work and are finished ushering them to and from their extracurricular activities, there isn't much time left at all. Be deliberate with that time. Make it special. Think back to the weeks leading up to your child's birth. I'm sure you didn't wish and pray that you would only be halfway present in their lives. Talk about their day and your day, help with homework, eat dinner together, play a game, go for a walk. Remember that one day your child will grow up and hopefully help care for you if and when the time comes. This is the time to model for your child how to be attentive to their loved ones.

Journal

_____

_____

_____

_____

_____

_____

_____

_____

_____

_____

_____

_____

_____

_____

_____

Write down things you like about each other.

Take some time to write down something you like about the other people in your family. If your daughter cannot write yet, you could talk about the things that you like about each other.

Hearing that other people like things about you helps boost your confidence and self-esteem. In today's world, having a strong sense of self-worth and self-confidence is important. Your perception of yourself is likely a reflection of what people told you when you were younger until you believed it enough to adopt those views, or different views for yourself.

Journal

_____

_____

_____

_____

_____

_____

_____

_____

_____

_____

_____

_____

_____

_____

_____

_____

_____

_____

_____

_____

_____

Write letters to family members, the old-fashioned way.

First, select a family member to write a letter to sometime this week. If possible, have your child write as much of the letter as possible, even if you hold his hand as he forms the words and sentences. For very small kids, drawing a picture or coloring a page also works well. Practice addressing the envelope and putting a stamp on it. Make a special trip to the post office where your child can mail the letter, or just put it in your mailbox and have them put the flag up. Always explain what you are doing during each step.

Writing physical letters and using the postal service to deliver them is becoming a lost art. It used to be a point of pride to have beautiful handwriting, but now most correspondence is via email, phone or text.

Still, even as adults we are thrilled when we receive a handwritten letter from a friend in the mailbox (instead of just bills and junk mail). When your child receives a letter or card in the mail that's addressed to her, make sure you make a big deal of the occasion and you'll realize the power of these personal correspondences. When your family member excitedly calls you to tell you they received a personal letter from your child, you both will recognize the payoff of this gesture.

Journal

_____

_____

_____

_____

_____

_____

_____

_____

_____

_____

_____

_____

_____

25

Make thank-you cards for teachers.

Have your child write or draw a thank-you card for his teacher. Send it to school during teacher appreciation week, or any time at all.

As educators who have spent time in the classroom, teaching can be an explicitly thankless job. Those charged with helping direct the growth and development of our youth are clearly undervalued according to their compensation, but sometimes also undervalued by parents and students. How many times did each of us tell our favorite teacher how awesome we thought they were when we were in school? This is an opportunity to tell someone who is most likely pretty amazing how special they are to us.

Trust me, it will brighten that educator's day and will probably be kept in a safe place for a long time for those days when they need a reminder.

Journal

_____

_____

_____

_____

_____

_____

_____

_____

_____

_____

_____

_____

_____

_____

_____

_____

_____

_____

Wow! 25 Weeks! Do you remember, in the beginning of the book, when I said we were committed to going through these exercises again with our daughter and for the first time with our son? Well, we all made it through, together! How did it go for you and your family? I hope you were able to take notes, along the way, which will allow you to revisit how you and your family felt in that moment. Another bonus to journaling your experience is being able to compare this journey with a future trip around the parenting gym. As what happened with our daughter, as our children get older, they will learn more and some experiences will fade. Revisiting these challenges well help our children to retain key information and understand the experiences in different ways as their understanding develops and changes.

Parenting can be quite an intentional and rewarding process. Some of the exercises in this book were designed for the children, some were geared toward the family, and others targeted only the parents. We hope that everyone in your family learned something new about themselves, about each other, and about your family. As parents, we understand that there are challenges to incorporating even the most basic addition to an already hectic schedule. These exercises encourage us to be intentional as parents and were designed to be easy to implement. As you interacted with your children and family in different ways over the past 25 weeks, we hope you have been inspired to incorporate some or all of the Exercises to Strengthen Your Parenting Muscles!

5 Books, 3 Authors, 1 Family

The Things I See: Scavenger Hunt
ISBN: 978-1-941592-01-4
Co-authors:
Chinenye O. Oparah and Kia M. Haselrig-Oparah
Published By: Raise the Bar Learning, L.L.C.
www.raisethebarlearning.com

Yum Yum! New Tastes are Fun!
ISBN: 978-1-941592-00-7
Author: Kia M. Haselrig-Oparah
Published By: Raise the Learning, L.L.C.
www.raisethebarlearning.com

The Science Behind It: Formulating Success At Any Age
ISBN: 978-0-578209-00-5
Author (Book Collaboration): Kemery C. Oparah
www.kemeryoparah.com

Parenting is a Verb: The Art of Unlocking Your Baby's Potential
ISBN: 978-1-941592-06-9
Authors: Chinenye O. Oparah & Kia M. Haselrig-Oparah
www.raisethebarlearning.com

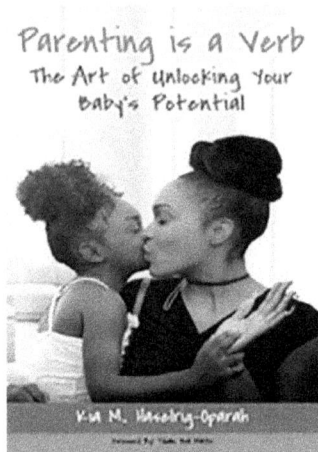

www.ingramcontent.com/pod-product-compliance
Lightning Source LLC
Chambersburg PA
CBHW071846020426
42331CB00007B/1870